# THE SEA BOOK

DK

# DIVE INTO A WATERY WORLD

The sea covers almost three-quarters of the Earth's surface. This immense body of water is home to an enormous variety of creatures, and is important to all life on land too. But the sea and its inhabitants are being damaged. This is not only sad, it is also a problem that affects the whole planet.

**Let's explore the sea and find out why it's so important.**

# OUR BLUE PLANET

If we look at planet Earth from far away in outer space, it looks very blue. This is because our planet is mostly covered in water. It is all this water that gives life to everything on Earth.

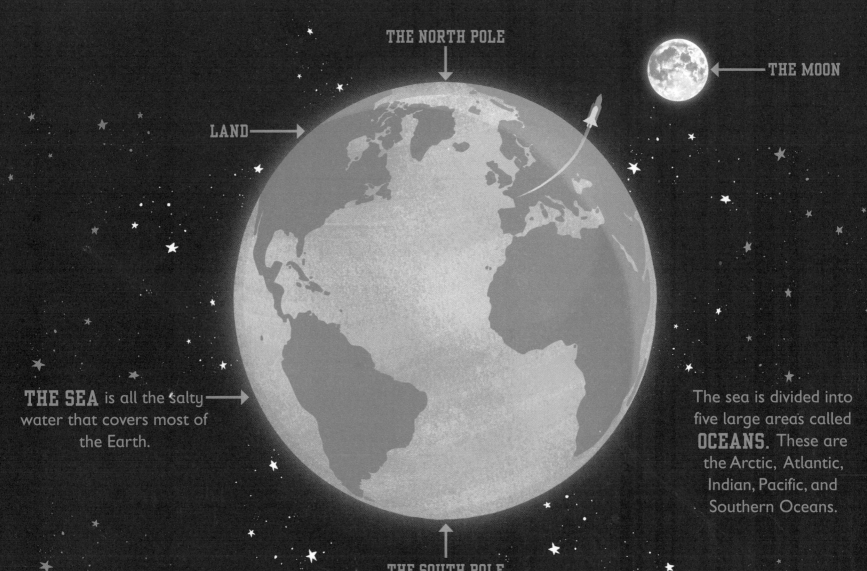

THE NORTH POLE

THE MOON

LAND

THE SEA is all the salty water that covers most of the Earth.

The sea is divided into five large areas called OCEANS. These are the Arctic, Atlantic, Indian, Pacific, and Southern Oceans.

THE SOUTH POLE

The sea is planet Earth's biggest habitat and it is home to many living things. **MARINE LIFE** describes all the animals and plants that live in the sea.

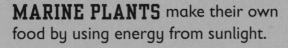

**MARINE PLANTS** make their own food by using energy from sunlight.

**MARINE ANIMALS** eat plants and other animals.

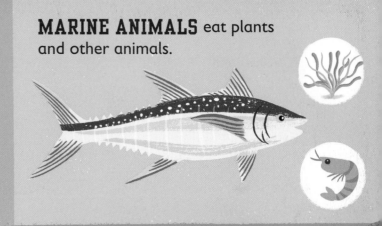

Even where you cannot see it, there is life in the sea. Just one drop of seawater contains thousands of tiny floating plants, animals, and other microscopic creatures called **PLANKTON**.

Plankton might be tiny, but it is very important because it is the base of every **FOOD CHAIN** in the ocean.

Lots of marine animals eat plankton.

Other bigger animals eat the plankton-eating animals.

**Shark**

Animals that eat other animals are called **PREDATORS** and the animals that predators eat are called **PREY**. The shark is the top predator in this food chain.

5

# WHAT DOES THE BOTTOM OF THE SEA LOOK LIKE?

Far from being flat, the sea floor is actually similar to the landscape we see above the waves. In the oceans, there are erupting volcanoes, deep trenches, and mountains taller than Mount Everest, the highest peak on land.

The sea is separated into four different zones:

**SUNLIT ZONE –** Many plants and sea creatures need warmth and light from the Sun to survive, so they live here, close to the surface.

**TWILIGHT ZONE –** Very little sunlight reaches down into water below 200m (650ft), so you won't find plants here. There are still plenty of animals, however, and many swim up to the sunlit zone at night to find food.

**MIDNIGHT ZONE –** Even though it is pitch black and cold, there are still fish and jellyfish living here, though fewer than in the zones above.

**THE ABYSS –** The deepest and darkest parts of the ocean are something of a mystery as few scientists have been able to explore water this deep. But some strange creatures have been found here.

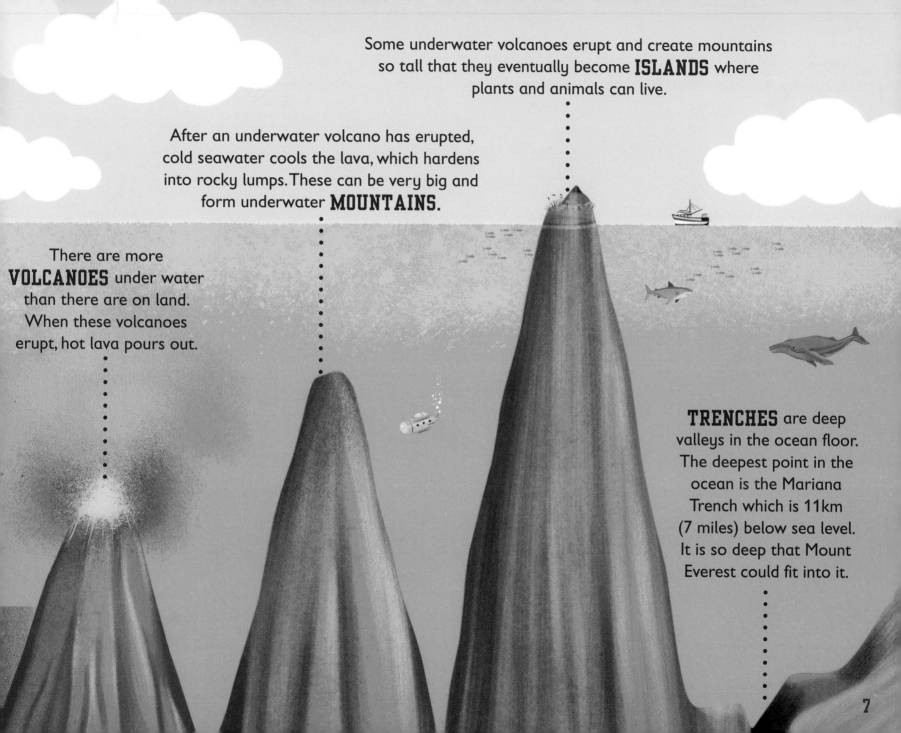

Some underwater volcanoes erupt and create mountains so tall that they eventually become **ISLANDS** where plants and animals can live.

After an underwater volcano has erupted, cold seawater cools the lava, which hardens into rocky lumps. These can be very big and form underwater **MOUNTAINS**.

There are more **VOLCANOES** under water than there are on land. When these volcanoes erupt, hot lava pours out.

**TRENCHES** are deep valleys in the ocean floor. The deepest point in the ocean is the Mariana Trench which is 11km (7 miles) below sea level. It is so deep that Mount Everest could fit into it.

# WHY IS THE SEA IMPORTANT?

We spend most of our time on land but we are always connected to the sea. We wouldn't be here without it. This is because the oceans, and the creatures in them, help to create the air we breathe, the water we drink, the food we eat, and much more.

## THE SEA CONTROLS OUR WEATHER

Seawater absorbs heat from the Sun. Ocean currents move this heat around the world, which affects the temperature in the air.

## THE SEA CREATES THE AIR WE BREATHE

Seaweed and plankton make over half of the oxygen that animals – including us – breathe in.

## THE SEA GIVES US FOOD

Fish are full of important nutrients, like protein. They provide an important source of food for people all over the world.

**Ocean currents** are like underwater winds that move water from one place to another.

## THE SEA GIVES US WATER

The oceans play an important role in the world's water cycle. Without the sea, we wouldn't have rain or water to drink.

The Sun heats the sea and turns water into **vapour.** Vapour rises and makes rain clouds.

## THE SEA ABSORBS CARBON DIOXIDE

Carbon dioxide is a gas that animals breathe out. We also create carbon dioxide when we burn fossil fuels such as oil and coal. Burning fossil fuels makes electricity and powers cars, but too much of it in the air harms the environment. The ocean and marine plants help by absorbing carbon dioxide from the air.

## THE SEA SUPPORTS AN ENORMOUS VARIETY OF LIFE...

9

# WHAT **LIVES** BENEATH THE WAVES?

Life is everywhere in the sea – from the sunlit ocean surface to the darkest depths. This makes it a fascinating, exciting, and very important place.

**Let's find out more about some of the creatures that make the sea their home.**

# PLENTY OF FISH IN THE SEA

When you think of the sea, the first animal you picture is probably a **FISH** that might look like the one you can see here. But fish come in all sorts of shapes and sizes, and they have special features for living under water.

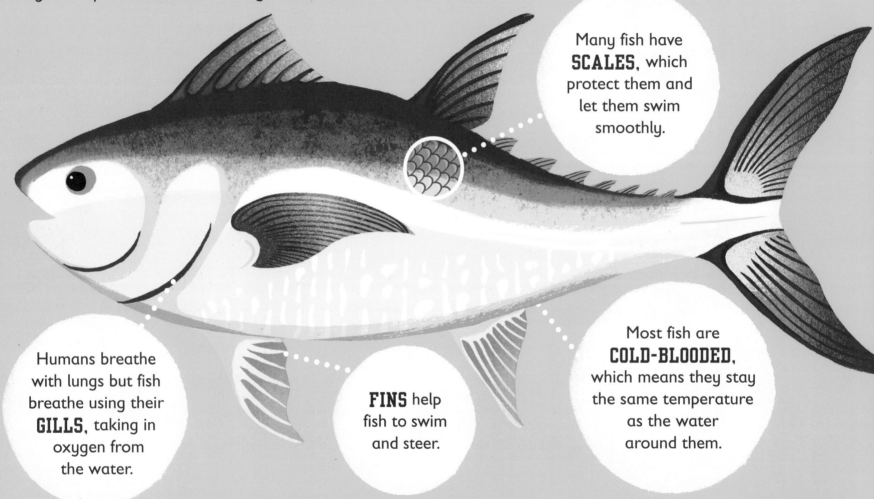

Many fish have **SCALES**, which protect them and let them swim smoothly.

Humans breathe with lungs but fish breathe using their **GILLS**, taking in oxygen from the water.

**FINS** help fish to swim and steer.

Most fish are **COLD-BLOODED**, which means they stay the same temperature as the water around them.

THERE ARE MORE THAN **33,000** SPECIES (TYPES) OF FISH. WHILE MOST OF THEM HAVE GILLS, FINS, AND SCALES, THEY ARE ALL VERY DIFFERENT...

## SOME FISH CAN FLY...

**FLYING FISH** use their wing-like fins to leap out of the ocean and glide through the air, helping them to escape from predators.

## SOME FISH CAN DANCE...

Male and female **SEAHORSE** couples dance together. Changing colour as they move, the couples swim side-by-side, linking tails and circling around each other.

## SOME FISH ARE FLAT...

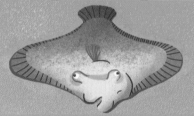

The flat body of a **FLATFISH** allows it to bury itself in the sand. Its sandy colour keeps it hidden from hungry sharks.

## SOME FISH ARE LONG...

**GIANT OARFISH** grow to at least 10m (33ft) long. Before people knew what they were, oarfish were thought to be dangerous sea serpents.

## SOME FISH ARE SPIKY...

**PUFFERFISH** can fill their stomachs with water, making themselves too round and spiky for predators to swallow.

## AND SOME FISH ARE VERY BIG...

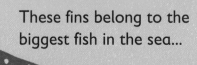

These fins belong to the biggest fish in the sea...

# WHAT IS THE BIGGEST FISH IN THE SEA?

Whale sharks are the biggest fish in the sea, but their favourite meal is the smallest of sea creatures – plankton. Whale sharks belong to a group of fish with a fierce reputation, but these huge **SHARKS** are gentle giants.

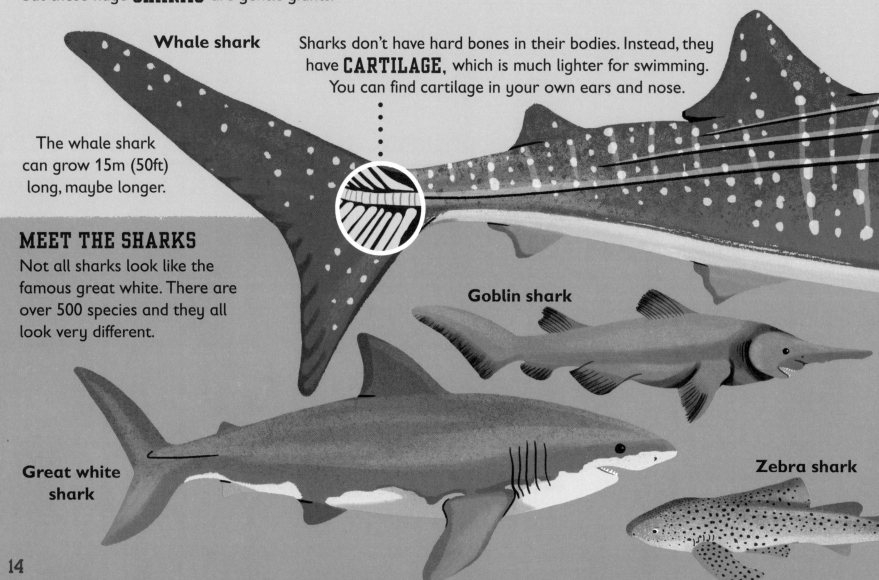

**Whale shark**

Sharks don't have hard bones in their bodies. Instead, they have **CARTILAGE,** which is much lighter for swimming. You can find cartilage in your own ears and nose.

The whale shark can grow 15m (50ft) long, maybe longer.

## MEET THE SHARKS

Not all sharks look like the famous great white. There are over 500 species and they all look very different.

**Goblin shark**

**Great white shark**

**Zebra shark**

All sharks are meat-eaters and their super senses, especially their fantastic sense of **SMELL**, make them experts at finding prey.

Sharks have **EARS** inside their bodies, but their hearing is much better than ours.

# RIGHT TOOL FOR THE JOB

These sharks have some strangely shaped heads that help them to find and catch prey.

Most sharks have five pairs of **GILLS**, but a few have six or seven. Some sharks, like the whale shark, have to keep swimming to breathe.

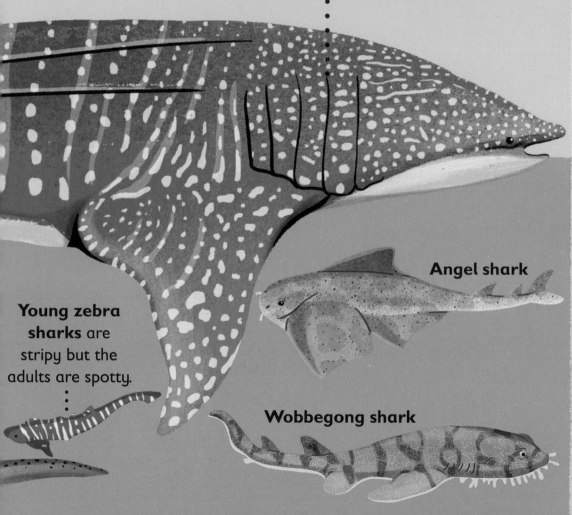

**Hammerhead sharks** pin down stingrays with their T-shaped heads. Their wide-set eyes give them excellent vision.

**Sawsharks** slash fish with their saw-like snout and sharp teeth.

**Young zebra sharks** are stripy but the adults are spotty.

**Angel shark**

**Wobbegong shark**

**Cookiecutter** sharks bite chunks out of large fish and dolphins, leaving them with a cookie-shaped bite mark.

# SCALY SWIMMERS

**REPTILES** are cold-blooded animals that have scales. They can't breathe under water so most of them live on land. However, there are a few that live in water and can hold their breath for a long time. Scaly swimmers that live in the sea are called marine reptiles.

A long, flat tail helps the iguana swim.

The iguana nibbles on seaweed with its sharp teeth.

The **MARINE IGUANA** is the only lizard that finds its food in the sea. When it comes above water, it does a big sneeze to blow away the build-up of salt in its blood, which it gets from its salty diet.

Its long claws help it grip onto rocks.

## OTHER MARINE REPTILES

**Saltwater crocodile**

**Sea snake**

**Sea turtle**

# THE LIFE CYCLE OF A SEA TURTLE

Female sea turtles come on land when it's time to lay their eggs, but males will never leave the sea once they enter it as a hatchling.

## 1.

Most turtle eggs hatch at night. **HATCHLINGS** rush from the sand into the sea, dodging crabs and birds that try to eat them.

## 2.

Young turtles go on a great adventure in the ocean, but where they travel in these early years is unknown. We call these the **LOST YEARS.**

An egg will hatch into a female sea turtle if the sand is warm, or a male if the sand is cool.

Green turtles eat seagrass and algae.

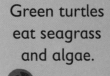

## 4.

When a female turtle is ready to **LAY EGGS**, she can travel thousands of miles to return to the same beach where she herself hatched.

## 3.

A sea turtle takes 10 to 15 years to grow into an **ADULT**. Adults spend most of their time in coastal waters where they find food.

# MEET THE MAMMALS

Most mammals give birth to their babies, need air to breathe, and are warm-blooded. This group of animals, which includes humans, is mostly found on land, although some mammals live in water. Aquatic mammals have **fins** and **flippers** for swimming, and thick, fatty **blubber** or special fur to keep them warm.

## DUGONGS

Also known as sea cows, dugongs spend their lives grazing on sea grass. These peaceful plant-eaters greet each other with kisses and keep their calves close to them for two years.

## BALEEN WHALES

Whales that don't have teeth are called baleen whales. Instead of using teeth to eat its food, a baleen whale has a mouth like a sieve, which filters food from the water.

A **blue whale** is a type of baleen whale and is the biggest animal in the world. It can grow up to 30m (100ft) long. That's even longer than the biggest dinosaur.

**Dolphins**

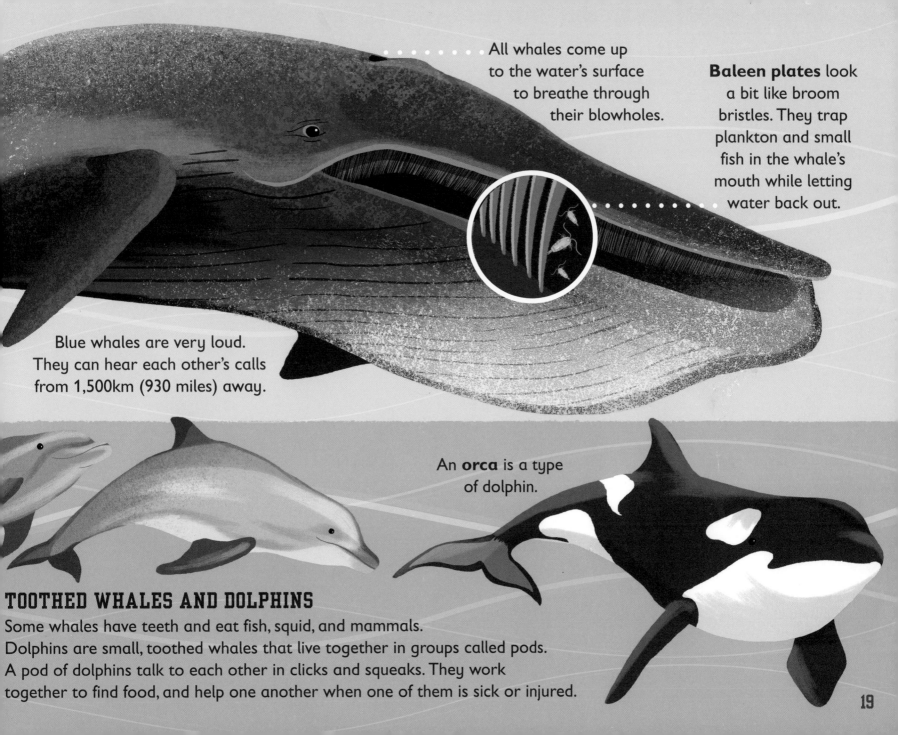

All whales come up to the water's surface to breathe through their blowholes.

**Baleen plates** look a bit like broom bristles. They trap plankton and small fish in the whale's mouth while letting water back out.

Blue whales are very loud. They can hear each other's calls from 1,500km (930 miles) away.

An **orca** is a type of dolphin.

## TOOTHED WHALES AND DOLPHINS

Some whales have teeth and eat fish, squid, and mammals. Dolphins are small, toothed whales that live together in groups called pods. A pod of dolphins talk to each other in clicks and squeaks. They work together to find food, and help one another when one of them is sick or injured.

19

# OTHER CURIOUS CREATURES

Most of the world's animals belong to a big group called **INVERTEBRATES**. Members of this group are mostly small and don't have backbones, which other large animals need to support their bodies. Instead, invertebrates have soft bodies and some have a hard shell to protect themselves.

**OCTOPUSES** have large heads, eight arms, and three hearts. As well as having a brain in its head, an octopus has lots of mini brains in its arms too!

Most octopuses can squirt black ink to confuse predators, and they are able to change their colour and texture to camouflage themselves.

The arms have suckers, which grip onto prey.

Octopus mothers guard their eggs for weeks without eating, eventually dying of starvation.

Octopuses can squeeze their soft bodies into tiny hiding places.

## STARFISH

Most starfish have five arms...

but some have more...

and some have arms so short they look like cushions! Starfish can regrow their arms if they lose one.

## JELLYFISH AND ANEMONES

Jellyfish and anemones may not have brains, but they do have tentacles that can give a nasty sting.

## CRABS AND LOBSTERS

These animals are protected by hard shells and have claws for capturing, crushing, and cutting their prey.

## SEA SLUGS

Sea slugs are brightly coloured to warn predators that they taste disgusting!

# THERE'S NO **PLACE** LIKE **HOME**

Just as there are a variety of places on land, the sea also has lots of different areas. There are hot areas, cold areas, deep, and shallow ones. Some places are brimming with colourful life and others are like enormous deserts. Across the sea, animals and plants depend on each other, as well as on where they live, to survive.

**Let's explore the places where marine animals live and see how they survive there...**

Lots of marine animals live on the **seashore**. Rock pools are homes to animals like sea anemones and starfish, which grip onto rocks so they don't wash away when the sea moves in and out.

# A LIFE ON THE ICE

The North Pole is located in the middle of the Arctic Ocean where it is extremely cold. Here lots of seawater freezes, making floating blocks of ice called **PACK ICE**. This floating ice is home to many marine animals. The **FOOD CHAIN** below shows how Arctic animals depend on the ice and each other for food and survival.

**Plankton** grows in and on the under-surface of pack ice.

**Krill** are small, shrimp-like animals that eat plankton.

**Cod** and lots of other fish eat krill.

**Narwhals** and **beluga whales** are types of toothed whales.

A narwhal has a single, long tusk, which is why it has become known as the unicorn of the sea.

Ringed seals have strong claws to make breathing holes in the ice.

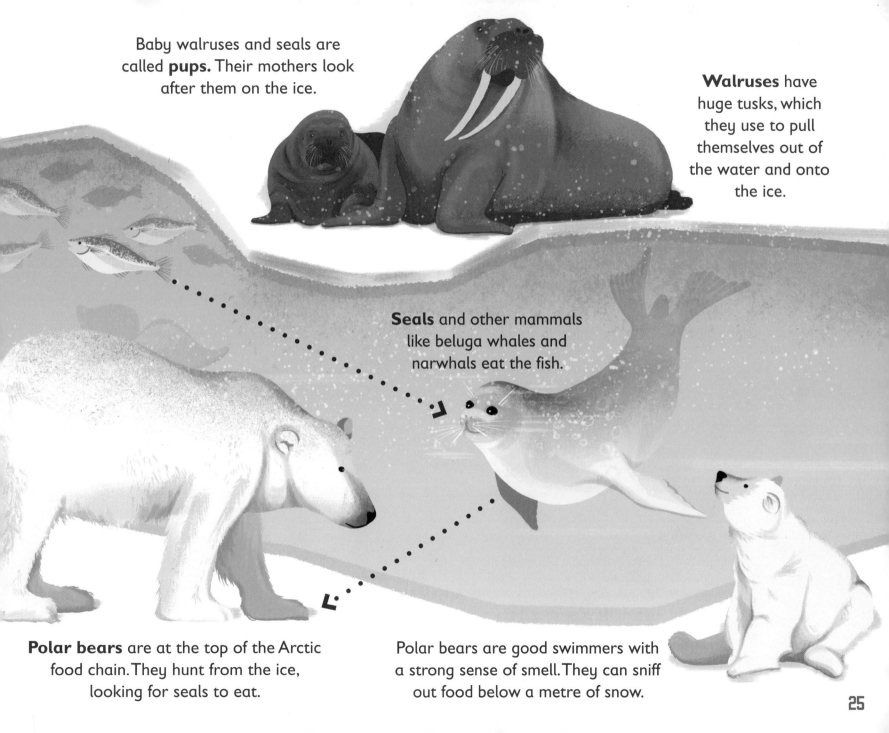

Baby walruses and seals are called **pups.** Their mothers look after them on the ice.

**Walruses** have huge tusks, which they use to pull themselves out of the water and onto the ice.

**Seals** and other mammals like beluga whales and narwhals eat the fish.

**Polar bears** are at the top of the Arctic food chain. They hunt from the ice, looking for seals to eat.

Polar bears are good swimmers with a strong sense of smell. They can sniff out food below a metre of snow.

25

# CORAL REEF CITY

Coral can be found in the tropics, where the seawater is warm, clear, and shallow. Like buildings in an underwater city, coral provides homes for thousands of marine animals. Coral reefs are bursting with so much life that scientists are discovering new species of animals there all the time.

## THE DAY SHIFT

In the day, the coral reef residents are out searching for food while dodging predators. Coral provides food for many colourful fish as well as a place for them to hide.

## WHAT IS CORAL?

While it might look like a plant, coral is actually made up of lots of tiny animals called polyps.

**Polyps** look like tiny anemones. Many of them live close together and make each large, rocky coral structure.

Some **parrotfish** feed on coral. They have strong, joined teeth like a bird's beak. Parrotfish use this "beak" to grind up the hard, rocky coral.

These **butterflyfish** spend their days nibbling at coral and searching for a partner who they will stay with for life. . . . . .

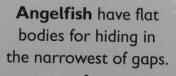

**Angelfish** have flat bodies for hiding in the narrowest of gaps.

# THE NIGHT SHIFT

Like a game of hide and seek, daytime colourful fish hide in the coral at night where they can sleep without being seen. Hungry reef sharks and other night-time predators are the "seekers". They come out at night to look for food.

Male adult angelfish are territorial. Young angelfish have different colours and markings so that the male adults don't confuse them with an adult rival who they might chase away.

**Whitetip reef sharks** eat fish, octopus, and crab. They have slender bodies to wriggle into narrow spaces and grab prey. . . . .

**Squirrelfish** come out of hiding at night. Their large eyes help them to spot prey in the dark. . . . .

At night, parrotfish create slimy cocoons that they sleep in. This might help stop predators from smelling and finding them.

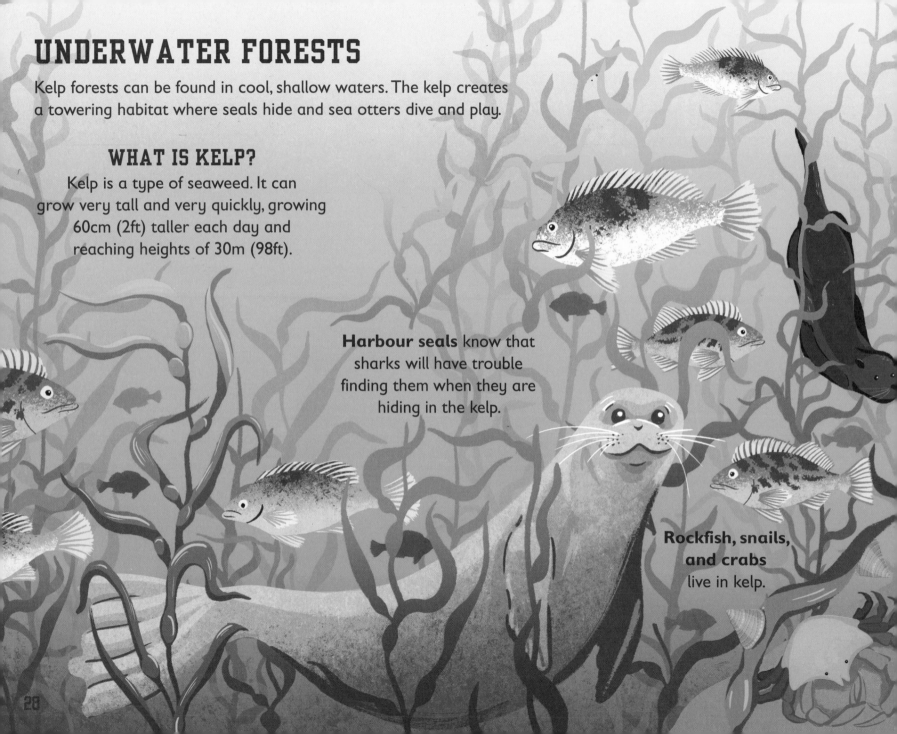

# UNDERWATER FORESTS

Kelp forests can be found in cool, shallow waters. The kelp creates a towering habitat where seals hide and sea otters dive and play.

## WHAT IS KELP?

Kelp is a type of seaweed. It can grow very tall and very quickly, growing 60cm (2ft) taller each day and reaching heights of 30m (98ft).

**Harbour seals** know that sharks will have trouble finding them when they are hiding in the kelp.

**Rockfish, snails, and crabs** live in kelp.

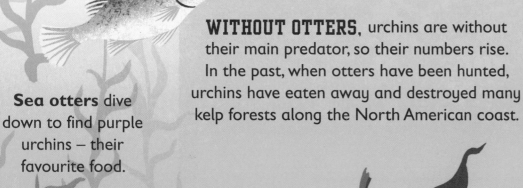

**Sea otters** dive down to find purple urchins – their favourite food.

**WITHOUT OTTERS**, urchins are without their main predator, so their numbers rise. In the past, when otters have been hunted, urchins have eaten away and destroyed many kelp forests along the North American coast.

**Sea urchins** are animals that eat lots of kelp. They have spikes for protection.

**WITH OTTERS** around, urchins stay under control. Today, sea otters are protected on the North American coast, and their numbers are rising. This means the kelp forests are recovering too, giving shelter and food to lots of other animals.

# THE BIG BLUE

Far from the shore, in the middle of the ocean, there are huge areas of open water. Near the shore there is plenty of food, but further out there is much less to eat. Animals that swim and drift here have almost nowhere to hide, so they have to find their own way to survive.

## THE DRIFTERS

Some animals float across the ocean waiting for food to drift by. Living this way doesn't require much energy, so animals can survive a long time without eating.

The **violet sea snail** makes a bubble raft to keep it floating on the ocean surface where it eats another drifter — the by-the-wind sailor.

The **Portuguese man-of-war** drifts using its gas-filled float, and has long, stinging tentacles to catch fish.

## THE VOYAGERS

Some animals travel thousands of miles across the ocean each year to get to the best places for finding food or having babies. This is called **migration.** Migrating marine animals often follow the ocean currents to help move them along their journey.

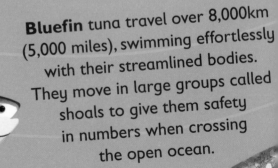

**Bluefin** tuna travel over 8,000km (5,000 miles), swimming effortlessly with their streamlined bodies. They move in large groups called shoals to give them safety in numbers when crossing the open ocean.

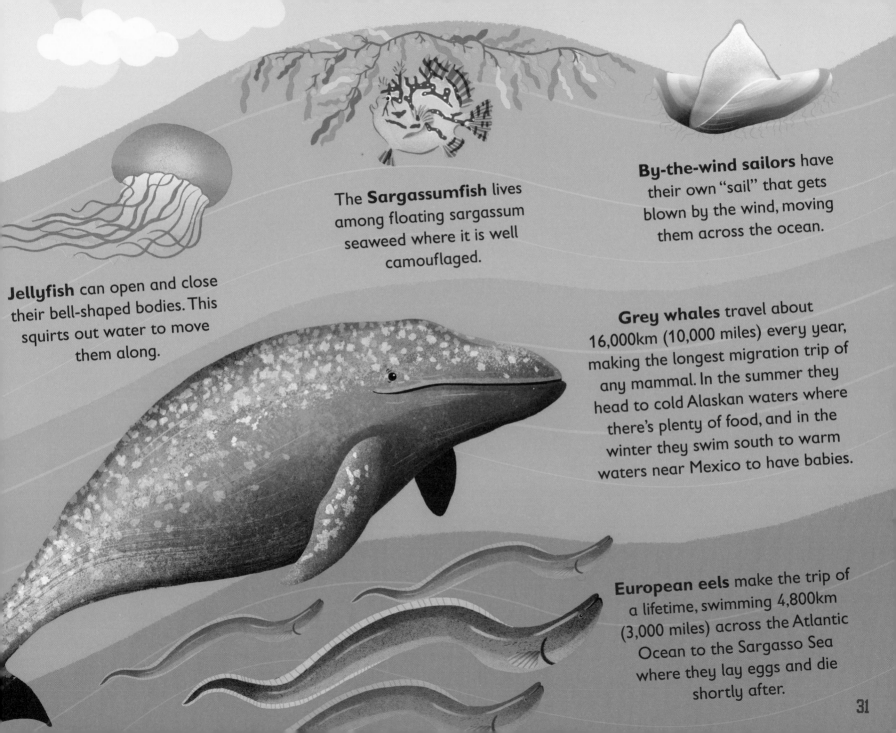

The **Sargassumfish** lives among floating sargassum seaweed where it is well camouflaged.

**By-the-wind sailors** have their own "sail" that gets blown by the wind, moving them across the ocean.

**Jellyfish** can open and close their bell-shaped bodies. This squirts out water to move them along.

**Grey whales** travel about 16,000km (10,000 miles) every year, making the longest migration trip of any mammal. In the summer they head to cold Alaskan waters where there's plenty of food, and in the winter they swim south to warm waters near Mexico to have babies.

**European eels** make the trip of a lifetime, swimming 4,800km (3,000 miles) across the Atlantic Ocean to the Sargasso Sea where they lay eggs and die shortly after.

31

# DARK AND DEEP

Deep in the ocean is a place like no other. Here, there is no natural light, it is very cold, and the weight of the water above creates immense pressure. Like a different planet, we have barely begun to explore the deep ocean and the strange creatures that live there.

This **viperfish** catches prey with its huge teeth, which are so big it can't even close its mouth. • • • • • • •

**Gulper eels** can swallow fish that are larger than themselves using their huge, flexible jaws and expanding stomach. • • •

• • • • Sponges draw in water to get the oxygen and food that they need. The **venus flower basket** is a sponge with a delicate, white skeleton made of the same material that is used to make glass.

## A HOME FOR LIFE

**Shrimp** couples live inside the venus flower basket. The male and female enter as small shrimps and grow too big to leave the sponge's woven walls. They stay together for life, cleaning their sponge home. In return, the sponge gives them food and protection.

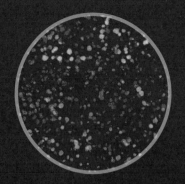

## DOES IT SNOW UNDERWATER?

No, but the remains of marine creatures sink from waters above like a shower of snowflakes. This is called **marine snow**.

Some animals glitter and glow in the darkness. This ability to create light is called **BIOLUMINESCENCE.**

Despite its scary name, the **vampire squid** is a peaceful animal that spends its life eating marine snow. When threatened, it turns its webbed arms back over its head like an inside-out umbrella. • • • • •

When the **atolla jellyfish** is under attack, it puts on a magnificent light display. This attracts other, bigger animals that may eat the attacker.

The **anglerfish's** fin extends over its head and acts like a fishing rod with a "glow" on the end to lure prey into its big mouth.

The **venus fly trap anemone** uses its tentacles to trap marine snow and small creatures to eat. • • • • •

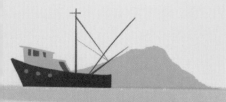

# WHAT'S THE CATCH?

Throughout the sea, animals and plants rely on each other to survive. But marine animals, plants, and their homes are facing problems that upset the natural balance. We once thought that the sea was too big for us to harm. We now know that humans have done more damage to the sea than we could ever have imagined possible.

**How is the sea being damaged?**

# TOO MANY BOATS, TOO FEW FISH

Fishing is important because fish are an essential part of many people's diet. But if too many fish are being caught too quickly, it creates a problem. When too many fish are taken out of the sea to eat, there are not enough left to breed and produce more fish. We call this **OVERFISHING**.

When there are fewer fish, it affects many other animals because it changes an entire food chain.

Overfishing causes the number and size of fish to decline. This is because the fish that are left behind are too young to lay eggs and are likely to be caught before they grow old enough to do so.

Trawling is a type of fishing that uses heavy nets. These can damage the seabed, destroying the places where animals find food and shelter.

Fishing can also be harmful when other, larger animals such as dolphins and sea turtles get caught in the net.

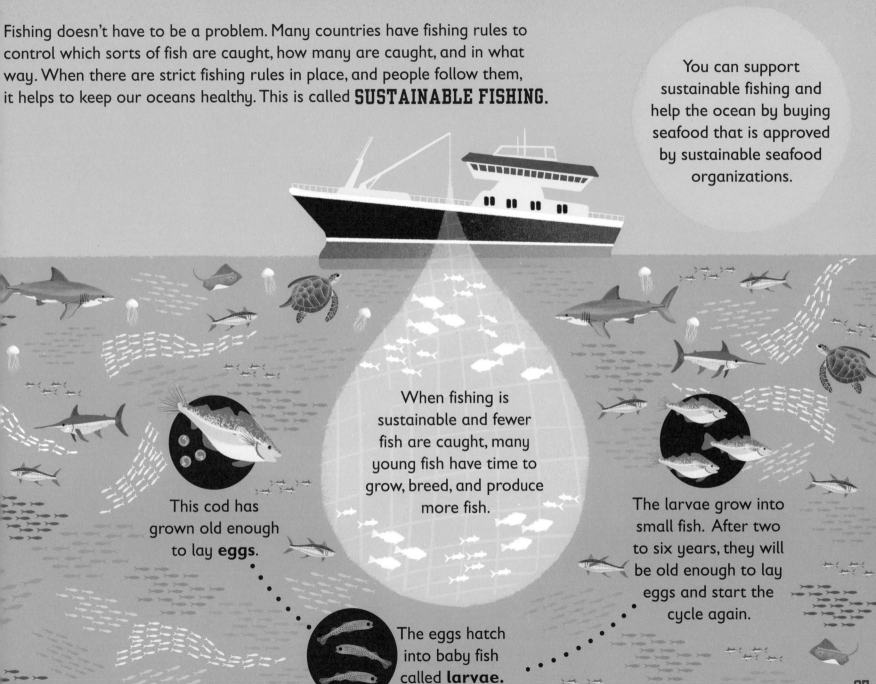

Fishing doesn't have to be a problem. Many countries have fishing rules to control which sorts of fish are caught, how many are caught, and in what way. When there are strict fishing rules in place, and people follow them, it helps to keep our oceans healthy. This is called **SUSTAINABLE FISHING**.

You can support sustainable fishing and help the ocean by buying seafood that is approved by sustainable seafood organizations.

When fishing is sustainable and fewer fish are caught, many young fish have time to grow, breed, and produce more fish.

This cod has grown old enough to lay **eggs**.

The eggs hatch into baby fish called **larvae**.

The larvae grow into small fish. After two to six years, they will be old enough to lay eggs and start the cycle again.

# CHANGING SEAS

The sea is getting warmer. This changes habitats and makes it difficult for marine animals to survive.

### WHY IS THE SEA GETTING WARMER?

To make electricity and use vehicles, we burn fossil fuels such as oil. Burning these creates a gas called **carbon dioxide.**

If there is lots of carbon dioxide in the atmosphere, planet Earth gets warmer. This is called **global warming.**

Global warming heats up the sea too and this can be harmful to the plants and animals that live there.

**Find out how global warming can affect the lives of some familiar animals...**

## MELTING ICE

As the sea gets warmer, it melts sea ice, destroying the homes of polar animals. This polar bear depends on sea ice for raising her young and hunting for seals. Without sea ice, she will find it hard to catch seals to eat.

## SEA LEVELS RISING

When polar ice melts, it creates more water, making sea levels rise. If this continues to happen, it could mean that many beaches become submerged. This sea turtle has travelled far to lay her eggs on the same beach where she hatched. She can't find the beach because it is now under water.

## WHITE SEAS

Warmer seas can make coral turn white, causing it to be very unhealthy or even die. This is called coral bleaching. These parrotfish can't find food because the coral that they like to nibble on is bleached. Like the parrotfish, lots of other animals on the reef will struggle to find food too.

# PLASTIC PROBLEMS

If we don't get rid of rubbish properly by recycling it or putting it in a bin, it can end up in the sea. Light plastic is a particular problem because the wind blows it into rivers and seas. Sadly, tonnes of rubbish, including plastic, has already got into the sea and it is harming marine life.

Plastic takes a very long time to break down. So when plastic gets into the sea, it can stay there and harm animals for many years, even if it breaks into tiny pieces.

Leatherback sea turtles eat plastic bags by mistake because they look a lot like their favourite food – jellyfish.

Albatrosses snap up food from the sea's surface. They accidentally catch plastic too and feed it to their chicks.

Many marine animals mistake plastic for food. If they eat a lot of plastic, it can block their stomachs. This stops them from feeling hungry and means they could starve.

After a long time, plastic does break into smaller parts. But these tiny bits of plastic get mixed up with plankton.

When plankton-eating animals swallow plastic, it then gets inside the meat-eaters who eat the plankton-eaters, eventually affecting the entire food chain.

Animals can get stuck in plastic bags and fishing nets. This can prevent them from being able to breathe or catch food.

# HOW CAN YOU HELP?

With the sea getting warmer, overfished and littered, it can all seem very scary. But when everybody does a little bit to help, we can make a big difference.

Go on a beach clean-up walk to pick up rubbish. Taking just two minutes to pick up litter will really help. Just remember to use gloves and have an adult's help.

The more we know about sea animals, the more we want to protect them. Visit the seashore, read about marine life, and share what you learn with your family, friends, and classmates.

Take litter home from the beach and recycle what you can.

Shells are homes to animals like the hermit crab. Leave plenty of shells on the beach and never buy shell souvenirs.

# LIVE WITH LESS PLASTIC

We once lived in a world where plastic didn't exist, but now we find it almost everywhere. It is very challenging to cut plastic out of our lives completely, but we should recycle what we do use. There are lots of simple ways to use less plastic and to reduce the amount that gets into the sea.

When you are out food shopping, help choose foods without packaging. Fruit and vegetables don't need to be in plastic, so just pick them up loose instead.

Say no to plastic straws. You might not need one or you can use paper straws instead.

Carry a reusable water bottle with you. Fill it up on-the-go to avoid buying drinks in plastic bottles.

Avoid using plastic cutlery and bring your own instead.

Take your own shopping bag with you that you can use again and again.

If you want to buy a hot drink when you're out, take a reusable mug with you. A lot of paper cups have a plastic lining that makes them difficult to recycle.

Rather than using plastic wrap that gets thrown away, pack your food in a container that can be used again, like a lunchbox.

43

# MAKE YOUR OWN SHOPPING BAG

Using your own shopping bag is a great way to stop using plastic ones. Making your own bag is fun and helps the animals in the sea too!

## YOU WILL NEED:

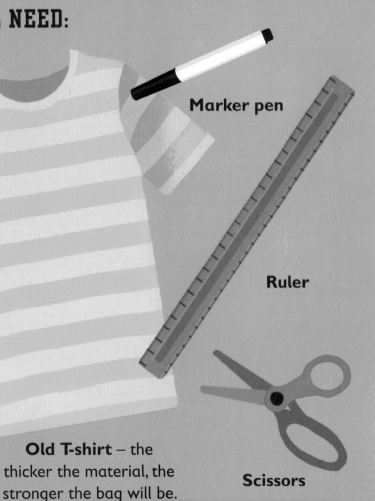

**Marker pen**

**Ruler**

**Scissors**

**Old T-shirt** – the thicker the material, the stronger the bag will be.

**1.**
Turn your T-shirt inside out. **Cut the sleeves off** with the help of an adult.

**4.**
With an adult's help, **cut slits** from the bottom of your T-shirt to your line to make a fringe.

Make the strands roughly 2cm (¾in) wide.

## 2.

**Cut an oval shape** around the neckline of your T-shirt – you will need an adult's help again.

## 3.

**Draw a line** 5cm (2in) from the bottom of the T-shirt. This is where the bottom of your bag will be.

Try **DECORATING** your bag! You could draw, sew, or paint on your favourite sea animal. That way, when you shop, you can remind yourself and others of the animals that you are helping to protect.

## 5.

**Double-knot** the front and back strands together until all of the fabric at the bottom of the T-shirt is tied.

## 6.

**Turn the T-shirt right side out** and you have a bag. Now you're ready to go shopping!

**Blue whales** were once hunted to near-extinction. Then people decided to help the whales and laws were introduced to ban whale hunting. Since then, their numbers have increased.

# A WAVE OF CHANGE

As a result of overfishing and pollution, humans are pushing the sea to its limit. It's time to protect these waters that we cannot live without. By doing what we can to help, we can give the sea a sustainable future to benefit both humans and animals.

**The sea is big enough for all of us to enjoy.**

# INDEX

**Author and Illustrator**
Charlotte Milner

**Editor** Violet Peto
**Consultant** Dr. Frances Dipper
**Senior Producer** Amy Knight
**Senior Producer, Pre-Production** Nikoleta Parasaki
**Jacket Coordinator** Francesca Young
**Managing Editor** Penny Smith
**Managing Art Editor** Mabel Chan
**Creative Director** Helen Senior
**Publisher** Sarah Larter

First published in Great Britain in 2019 by
Dorling Kindersley Limited
80 Strand, London, WC2R 0RL

A CIP catalogue record for this book
is available from the British Library.
ISBN: 978-0-2413-5537-4

Printed and bound in China

A WORLD OF IDEAS:
SEE ALL THERE IS TO KNOW

www.dk.com

DK would like to thank
Caroline Hunt for proofreading.

## ABOUT THE AUTHOR

Charlotte Milner creates books with playful designs to bring important information to young readers. Her first book, **The Bee Book,** explores the world of bees and how they fulfil a vital role in our ecosystem.